Beyond All Bearing

Beyond All Bearing

Susan Delaney Spear

RESOURCE *Publications* • Eugene, Oregon

BEYOND ALL BEARING

Copyright © 2018 Susan Delaney Spear. All rights reserved. Except for brief quotations in critical publications or reviews, no part of this book may be reproduced in any manner without prior written permission from the publisher. Write: Permissions, Wipf and Stock Publishers, 199 W. 8th Ave., Suite 3, Eugene, OR 97401.

Resource Publications
An Imprint of Wipf and Stock Publishers
199 W. 8th Ave., Suite 3
Eugene, OR 97401

www.wipfandstock.com

PAPERBACK ISBN: 978-1-5326-3740-7
HARDCOVER ISBN: 978-1-5326-3741-4
EBOOK ISBN: 978-1-5326-3742-1

Manufactured in the U.S.A.

For Bruce,
Emily, Vanessa,

& Peter—
Always

Contents

List of Illustrations | x
Acknowledgements | xi

Prologue
Invocation in Ordinary Time | 1

Vacant Blue

Chores | 4
Wild Traveler | 5
Behind the Wheel | 6
Forty Julys | 8
Fried Mush and Maple Syrup | 9
Vacant Blue | 10
Advent | 11
A Matter of Participles | 12
Foreshadows | 14

Saints and Such

"Where Two or Three Are Gathered. . ." | 16
Crescent Glow | 17
Old Ralph | 18
Vespers | 20
After the Interment | 21
. . . Yet Not Consumed. . . | 22
One Narrow Row | 24
Ode to Twins | 26
Easter Lament | 27

The Rancher's Tale | 28
Undercut | 29
Pricey Recipe | 30
Salt Water | 31
Laughter | 32
Check Them Out | 33
Season Tickets | 34
Outliers | 35
Blue Irises | 38
Aftermath of a Miracle | 39
Sunday Morning | 40
Hell-Bent | 42

Priorities

Leaving | 44
Mac and Cheese | 45
Defying Nature | 46
String Theory | 47
The Memory of Her Melody | 48
The Lovers' Knot | 49
Priorities | 50
Live Life Away | 51
Rosary 2.0 | 52
Through the Window | 53
Summer's End | 54

Where Dreams Comingle with Dust

Twilight | 56
Dust | 57
Faces of the Enemy | 58
Royal Revenge | 59
Your Name Is Seth | 60
A Narrative in Need of Words | 61
Fool | 63
Occupied | 64
Lilac Gowns | 65

Mosca Pass Trail to the Great Sand Dunes | 66
Rattled | 67
Return | 68
Meteor | 69
Epistle | 70
A Word | 71

Beyond All Bearing

Turning | 74
Honeysuckle | 75
Like the Wedding Supper of the Lamb | 78
Actuary Tables | 79
the thin place | 80
Paper Whites / December | 81
Crossing | 82
Tender | 84
Rainlight | 85
Consider These Lilies | 86
Beyond All Bearing | 87
"Concentric Moon" by Patricia Russell | 88

Illustrations

"Concentric Moon" by Patricia Russell
The eponymous poem "Beyond All Bearing" was written in response to the pencil sketch "Concentric Moon" by Patricia Russell

Acknowledgements

The author acknowledges with gratitude the following publications which first published many of these poems, some in earlier iterations.

823 on High: "Wild Traveler," "Easter Lament," and "Aftermath of a Miracle"

Academic Questions: "String Theory," "Royal Revenge," and "A Word"

Angle: "Turning," and "Season Tickets"

Anglican Theological Review: "Invocation in Ordinary Time"

The Christian Century: "Wind and Flame"

Commonweal: "Emmaus"

Dappled Things: "After the Interment," "Through the Window," and ". . . Yet Not Consumed. . ."

Don't Just Sit There: "Faces of the Enemy," "Twilight," "Old Ralph," and "Ode to Twins"

eVerse Radio: "Meteor," "Honeysuckle," "Actuary Tables," "Tender"

The Lyric: "Summer's End," and "The Lovers' Knot"

FUNGI Magazine: "Pricey Recipe"

Measure: "Behind the Wheel"

Mezzo Cammin: "Lilac Gowns," "Priorities," "A Matter of Participles," and "Rattled"

The Nervous Breakdown: "Crescent Glow"

Peacock Journal: "Angles," "Occupied," "Vespers," and "Blue Irises"

The Raintown Review: "Fool," and "Salt Water"

Relief: "Rainlight"

The Rocky Mountain Anthology: "Epistle"

The Rotary Dial: "Forty Julys"

Verse Wisconsin: "Defying Nature"

Women's Voices for Change: "Turning" (reprint from *Angle*) and "Paper Whites/December"

"The Lovers' Knot" won Honorable Mention in the Denver Women's Press Club Unknown Writers' Contest in the spring of 2010.

"Like the Wedding Supper of the Lamb" was a finalist in the 2016 *String Poet* contest.

PROLOGUE

An Invocation in Ordinary Time

Sing, Muse,
in common time

on the upbeat
of the sun

Cry, morning's
mourning dove

Chant, mossy
onyx rocks

Seek, osprey,
swoop and prey

Fling, red-
winged blackbird,

melodies
between the green

Squeak, smooth
pinewood floors

Crumble, loaf
of humble grain

Buoy my heart,
watered wine

Crash, waves,
erase my traces

Croak, frogs
an evensong

Sink, ancient
orange one

into the blue,
blackening sea

Come, Holy
Ghost, hum

in common places
Prove to me

your extraord-
inary graces.

Vacant Blue

Chores

I ran down Belmar Street to cross the highway
all by myself. This was a big girl mission.
I held the note you wrote up for the clerk.
Coins clattered. She read, she clicked her tongue,
dilly-dallied for a minute—stalled,
then handed me the shiny pack of Winstons.
My heart beat hard, my errand halfway done.
With pride I clutched the cellophane-wrapped prize
and backed out through the squeaky, wooden door.
Pebbles flew like sparks behind my Keds.
A Corvair screeched. Its bumper grazed my leg
and stopped. I eyed the driver through the glass.
She shook her head and laid it on the wheel.
Oh, no! Mommy's cigarettes!
My heartbeat halted; my lungs forgot to breathe.
Palms together, Winstons in between,
I mouthed the words "*I'm sorry, sorry, please. . . .*"
I shuddered, then I ran. I never told you.
I did my lethal best to win your love.

Wild Traveler

I rip the yellowed newsprint
from your German china bowl
and find mere shards, the fragments
of a once unbroken whole.

I trace a fractured rose
imposed on white and lavender
and see the pattern you chose
is stamped "Wild Traveler."

Intently searching for
a more revealing clue,
I rummage in a drawer
to find a print of you.

Your eyes and lips and nose
are startlingly my father's,
your waistline—mine, but those
likenesses are all it offers.

I am your last grandchild,
the one you never knew.
Were you fragile, sharp, and wild?
Am I at all like you?

Behind the Wheel

You say yes, I say no, you say
Stop and I say go, go, go...

"Hey, Ma, I heard you singing this old Beatle's
song and thought I'd pop around and join you."

    Alone with John, Paul, George, and Ringo,
    I shiver, pounding the steering wheel.

"Hear those birds? I used that chirping sample
on my CD....*blackbird singing in the dead...*

    "You can't drop in whenever.
      You don't get to choose."

"Remember when the DJ played
Twist and Shout? We danced at the reception."

    He sat shot gun, reaching out to squeeze my shoulder.
    Tears sprinted down my face.

"Ah, Ma. What's the matter? *Nothing is real.*
Nothing to get hung about," he sings.

    "'What's the matter' you say? The matter is
    I forgot that dance, then you show up."

"Come on! Teaching you to twist was great.
Lend me your ears and I'll sing you a song..."

    "You fell out of time. You are dead.
      Now act dead. Stop showing up."

He fades a shade or two and checks his phone.
I search his eyes. They blur over.

> "Hey, I only meant today.
> Not everyday. Not for always."

His singing dims, "*songs of laughter, shades of earth,
. . . call me on across the universe. . .*"

> "Oh, no. . . '*I don't know why you say goodbye
> I say hello.*' Hello, hello. . .?"

Forty Julys

It is July 1974:
four friends, a New York beach, and fireflies.
We swear we will be close forever and a day,
mountain roads, deer, and singing leaves,

four friends, a New York beach, fireflies,
transistor radios and talk of boys.
On mountain roads, under emerald leaves,
we chat on about our future lives.

Over the radio's hum, we talk of boys,
mosquito bites, Bactine, and suntan lotion.
We chat on about our future lives,
college plans, our older selves as wives,

more mosquito bites, *Let's try Calamine.*
I hide my fear of summer's forward motion
and July's dwindling days, no longer mine.
Gazing at the Adirondack sky,

I sense the sting that life and love might bring
and memorize that Adirondack blue.
(We swore we would be close forever and a day,
but that was years ago—forty Julys—)

Fried Mush and Maple Syrup

You winked and raised your
index finger to your lips.
The lard spit; I jumped.
You glanced over your shoulder.
You spooned cold yellow squares
into the cast iron pan.
Pale yellow turned to gold,
the edges crisped and browned.
You carefully lifted the squares
onto each white plastic plate.
Slice the butter you said
and handed me the knife.
I put two cool cubes
on fried corn meal squares
and watched them melt, pool
and swim toward the edges.
You removed Aunt Jemima's cap
and lifted her glass body.
We sat on the floor
watching black and white cartoons.
You whispered, *Don't tell Mommy
I fried mush for breakfast.*
I chewed that sticky secret,
so tender, crisp, and rich.

Vacant Blue

I race through florescent terminals
lugging my load. I fly
above green squares of wheat
through vacant blue, wondering how
I, for fifty years unblessed,
Can conjure love to ease
you into rest? As neon
spikes and dips monitor arrhythmic
beats and fitful, shallow breaths,
you lie oblivious this night.
I place my hand on
yours. It is still warm.
I study your high cheekbones,
your closed eyes, your hair,
too short, your double chin.
Our breath mingles. A second
hand marks time as red
flashing spikes and dips smooth
into two straight lines, traveling
left to right ad infinitum.
I say...*though I walk*
through the valley of shadow . . . .
I will fear no evil,
*Thou art with me...*I
brush your forehead. My fingertips
trace your cheek. The only
word I know is grace
to name this thing that
fills love's empty place.

Advent

The trees are empty, daylight wanes.
December air hangs cold and blue.
I stand on fallow, frozen ground,
and dream fresh dreams of Earth made new.

In my dreams, I'm always warm,
and lilac petals fall like snow.
I walk a gentle path with friends
I'd lost or grieved for long ago.

In my dreams, it's always light—
unsullied brightness never ends.
No evening shadows bring a chill;
no silent, somber dusk descends.

In my dreams, I wear no scars.
Old injuries have left no trace.
Like an oak, I stand up straight,
and as a willow, bend with grace.

But on this broken afternoon
in winter's unforgiving cold,
promises are overdue,
and unborn dreams too great to hold.

A Matter of Participles

variations on a line by Joslyn Green

Loving
matters
more
than
being
(loved,

loved,
loving)
Being
matters
less than
more. . .

more
loved
than
loving
Matters
being

equal

being
more
matters
(loved,
loving)
than. . .

more than
being
Loving
more
Love
matters,

matters
than...
loved:
Being
more
loving

Loving matters
more than
being loved.

Foreshadows

Jamaica Plain, July 2009

Tonight belongs to grieving.
There's no more in between.
Evening's light is leaving.
My son unlocks the screen.
I do not beg them stay.
They must be on their way.

The sun will run its course
and leave me here tonight.
It shoulders no remorse,
nor is my son contrite.
Assured and passing through,
they both have work to do.

I'll wait here in the dark.
My traveling days are done.
Tonight, the sky is stark.
There'll be no midnight sun.
Grief's countenance is stern,
not easily unlearned.

Saints and Such

Where Two or Three Are Gathered...

After Anne Porter (1911-2011)

A breeze breathes in and out the screen tonight.
A pearl of moon hangs just above
the maple leaves and spreads its quiet light
across my desk where copies of your poems
lie strewn, my favorites annotated.
A glass of pinot noir has left a stain
on page sixteen. Irreverent. Intimate.
I can see you, Anne, squinting to study
Millet's "Farmyard," your soul stirred by light.
A light unlike the brashness of the sun,
a *radiance, colorless*, that paints a *patch*
upon the *floor*. Touched by Millet's *small moon*
and the painting's shadows, you took pen
in hand, giving thanks, line by line,
for his scene, *hushed under the moon*.
Anne, can you see me at my desk
tonight, counting syllables and sipping
wine in my own patch of lesser light?

Crescent Glow

A slice of moon bleeds blue on wind-swept snow
and bares my secret in its lambent rush.
Short angled shadows stage a midnight show.
A slice of moon bleeds blue on wind-swept snow,
exposing me beneath its crescent glow.
My best-kept secret, naked in night's hush.
A slice of moon bleeds blue on wind-swept snow
and makes light of my secret in its rush.

Old Ralph

Music was Ralph's love. Late at night she lingered
beneath the touch of practiced, agile fingers.
In his living room stood two pianos,
an electric organ and one of those
antiquated pumpers. Students played
duets with Ralph each week. They often stayed
past their sixty minutes, playing hymns
or Bach until the setting sun's light limned
their music through the window to the west.
The teacher only broke the music's spell
to stir his bubbling soup a or give a yell
to shoo an errant sheep from off the steps.

One new moon night, a Chevy slowed then stopped.
The hoodlum who rode shotgun took a drag
and nodded at the farm, "That guy's a fag."
"Hey, let's have some fun. . . Let's scare the shit
Outta old Ralph," the driver said. "We'll git
him good," they cackled. "It's darker 'round back."
They crawled up the drive, swallowing their laughter.
One shouted "Faggot!" then beat down the door,
ransacking cupboards, plates breaking on the floor.
Ralph lay wide-eyed, frozen in his fear.
"Get outta bed and fight us, you old queer!"
One hood hammered on the grand piano,
"Let's get our asses outta here. Let's go!"
The driver sneered: "What a fucking joke."

Ralph heard their wicked laughter, their tires spinning,
and from nowhere, a soprano singing:
Sheep may safely graze and pasture
where a shepherd guards them well.
His blood raced through his arteries and veins
which, within minutes, could not contain
the rising pressure—suddenly—a stroke.

Ralph no longer moved his lips to pray.
His fingers, rendered useless, did not play.

Vespers

Now they stand, between two steepled pines
which face the north side of the country house
where for years, their hours and days espoused
the cause of always and silently entwined.
Twilight slides between green snowy needles
and limns their wrinkled faces from the west,
as April robins, two neighbors, and one guest
hush themselves inside this spare cathedral.
She wears the color of Hawaiian sand.
he, a jacket matching hers, and bolo tie.
The septuagenarians comply
And play into love's patient, proffered hand.
For years, their vows were tacit but unbroken.
Tonight, words curl in cold spring air, spoken.

After the Interment

The husband eats a slice of cherry pie,
fumbling with his napkin and his fork.
He searches for a way to say good bye,
sitting, sipping coffee from his spoon.

Fumbling with his napkin and his fork,
he puts one dimpled cherry in his mouth
and sips burnt coffee from a shiny spoon.
He bumps the knife. It clatters to the floor.

He rolls the sugared fruit around his mouth
And thinks, *I'm glad I didn't order a la mode.*
Struggling, he picks the knife up from the floor,
well-dressed, a bit unsteady, and alone.

I'm glad I didn't order a la mode.
The waitress asks, *More coffee, sir?*
Pin-striped, a bit unsteady, and alone,
he nods, *Today, I'll take it black.*

She deftly pours. *Anything else?*
There is no fitting way to say goodbye.
No, Ma'am. I'm satisfied.
He finishes the slice of cherry pie.

. . . Yet Not Consumed. . .

This is the gospel truth.
I knew her then, ten
years or so ago.
She claimed that she had seen
a common thorny bush
and caught an inkling of the holy.
Bemused friends shrugged,
but she swore by what she saw
and slipped off her sensible
size six shoes
to walk barefoot on the ground.
Neither the suck of mud,
nor the grip of ice on sole,
nor the sharp shards of rocks,
nor the sun-fried sidewalk
could convince her otherwise.
A fleeting decade later
I see her most mornings
as she wanders the trail
beside the shallow creek.
A dun-colored hoodie
drapes her close-cropped hair.
Ankle pants, the shade
of dried autumn cattails,
end at her naked feet,
the flesh browned and thickened,
the toes well-rounded.
When she moves, she moves
as if she's standing still.

Her eyes, the color of ash,
flash at the first sight
of crocuses and aspen shoots.
Although I knew her then
and I know her now,
I run past her on the right
wearing my neon Nikes
without a sideways glance
or a hand lifted in hello.
In my empty belly
grows a growling yearning
to see a scrubby bush,
and to see, no, to know:
that scrubby bush is burning.

One Narrow Row

> "The word of the Lord was rare in those days;
> visions were not widespread." 1 Samuel 3:1

The American imagines a mountain of rice
from which she scoops while the gaunt wait
politely, standing straight in tidy rows.
A wrinkled man brings nameless Chinese children,
and abandoned newborns mewl on windowsills.
She envisioned this world before she'd seen this world.

The woman prays for a purpose in this world
where air hangs like ice and people dream of rice,
where expressionless faces gaze through windows
obscured by ash. Empty-eyed, they wait.
The indecipherable sounds of children
echo to her down the village rows.

Unbridled faith compels her down gray rows
into a famished, honest-to-god world
where flesh clings tightly onto thin-boned children,
where bent women cluck, counting grains of rice,
where old men squat, smoke, tell jokes and wait,
and raw winds penetrate the doors and windows.

The once-blue paint peels from the wooden windows.
All Linjiang's alleys narrow to one row
of tears and ash. The fiery woman waits:
I dreamed this row, this alley, this world:
A village void of heat and toys and rice.
She stoops to touch the cheeks of children

without pencils, without parents. These children
woo her down the lanes lined with blue windows.
A hired man beside her hauls the rice,
one hundred pounds, as they limp the rows,
and a translator gives words to this old world
as they caravan each day. The empty wait.

The villagers of Linjiang do not know they wait,
They do not hope for healthy babies, happy children,
They cannot see through grimy windows.
They do not rage against this out-of-order world.
They live and move politely in their rows,
dreaming unvoiced dreams of pearly rice.

She will not wait, for Linjiang's windowsills
Are stained by death, and children shiver in rows.
In this world, her faith moves mountains of rice.

Ode to Twins

Barren moons,
We've wept.

Cells,
Multiply.

Fingers,
Form whorls.

Hands,
Seize tomorrow.

Ineffable pair,
Hang on.

Easter Lament

Monday, Holy Week,
a child died, limbs and laughter—
now soot and bits of bone.

Alleluias trip
on my tongue. The scent of lilies
disturbs my senses.

Extinguish the light.
Let's sit alone together
in cold, dim silence.

I know: Christ is raised—
but, please, no resurrection
hymns today, no praise.

The Rancher's Tale

On the table between Charlie and me
under the *Denver Post*, I saw a pamphlet.
Green letters read "Congestive Heart Failure."
"Are you in any pain?" Bruce asked.
Charlie laid his hand above his heart
and shook his head, indicating *no*.
Noiselessly a nurse appeared. "I'll be back
to take you for a walk, Mr. Tannin."
Bruce cleared his throat. "Let's hold hands and say
A prayer."
                      Charlie bowed his head, his eyes open.
His hands were warm. As we stood to go
he raised his palm and said, "Do you... like stories?"
"Sure, Charlie. We like jokes." I sat back down.
Charlie breathed with effort, "A man died.
His wife... went to... the news... paper... and said,
'Please print... Sven died.' The editor... replied...
'You get three... more words... for the same... amount.'
The woman thought... a minute... then she said,
'OK. Then... please add... Boat for Sale.'"
Charlie gasped and gulped the oxygen.
We laughed, disquieting the evening peace.

Undercut

When her husband's blood filled up with cancer,
the doctors dredged the marrow from his bones.
As months dragged on they waited, but no answer.
Starved for life, she left him on his own.

She met a man who matched her lust for life.
They built a house where grief would not belong.
Together they beat out the dust of death,
while her ailing husband's blood grew strong.

Cancer's shadow held its breath and stalked,
and when the time was ripe, it got her gut.
Two men rubbed shoulders at her grave and balked
to see her life, at forty, undercut.

Pricey Recipe

She splurged on cognac and ignored the cost
of delicate, thin crimini mushrooms.
They were still his favorites, she assumed.
No short cuts, or subtle flavors might be lost.
She tenderly sliced the beef against its grain,
diced a sweet, white onion, and sliced fresh shallots.
While sizzling peppered chunks enticed her palate,
the bubbling noodles fogged the windowpane.
She poured in brandy, which mustn't get too hot,
Stirred it patiently, then added stock.
A spoon of mustard lent a savory shock.
Sipping, she drizzled wine around the pot.
But, his tastes had changed, his lips had wandered off,
while she was cooking him a stroganoff.

Salt Water

They're in the throes of it,
the whispered blows of it
the nobody-knows of it
the so—it—goes of it
the intimate assault of it
the it's—your—fault of it
the stinging salt of it
the familiar default of it.

He wields the blame of it,
the red-hot game of it.
She assumes the shame of it,
the quotidian same of it.
They plunge into its undertow—
and swim the sea of homemade woe.

Laughter

You were decades late, God.
I grew weary waiting
on your lavish promises
of children as numerous as stars.
With each hollow year
my skin mirrored more the ripples
on the wind–blown sand.
I overheard your words
This time next year
and choked back a scoff.

When my breasts began
to fill, the sign of
a womb in use,
I dared not tell a soul—

but when I felt life flutter
I hid my toothless grin,
the inconceivable now obvious.
You arrived tardy,
God, just in time.
Pain washed in like waves.
The baby squalled, the Negev's
sand swirled skyward,
and countless stars laughed.

Check Them Out...

. . . bedecking wooden pews,
the women fidget tensely; husbands snooze.
You know their type: they slither up a cross,
and for forty days they paint a gloss
of sacrifice onto their cozy lives.
John forgoes Starbucks, yet he survives
by drinking delicate imported tea.
Jan swears off chocolate, a panacea
for her mortal sins. Bob forfeits wine,
and sips a bit of brandy when he dines.
Trish won't indulge in water cooler natter;
she'll spend her wagging words on weighty matters.
That teen gives up TV (which wastes his time)
for video games and solving virtual crimes.
For Lent last year, Barbara gave up sex—
No one's surprised her husband's now her ex.
The balance on Scott's Visa screams excess,
so for Lent: American Express.
Ann sacrifices meat, but she'll get by on
salmon, lobster, trout and jumbo prawn.
Roger proclaims that he'll stop smoking pot.
He's stocked with Valium; he'll need a lot.
Check them out: they're stylishly adorned
with chic and costly crowns of thorns.

Season Tickets

She did not cry at his memorial,
not when the bagpipe's dirge prickled her skin,
not even when she watched her daughters' tears
forge trails down their cheeks and off their chins.
She had grieved each loss along the way
And so she gathered up his coins and cash,
his unused Starbucks cards, and bought us lunch
and coffee from his scattered night-stand cache.
She did not weep, she told me, when she dried
her hands on his worn towel hanging askew.
But when their scheduled concert date arrived,
an untapped sadness fell and tears broke through.
She said it was the drive, alone, at night,
the tender cello, and his seat on her right.

Outliers

"... Tamar... Rahab... Ruth... the wife of Uriah..."
Matthew 1: The Genealogy of Jesus

Tamar

Judah coldly threw me from his house,
so I waited and conceived a plan
to carry on the name of my dead spouse.
I donned a linen veil to lure that man,
my father-in-law, Judah, as he passed.
Blinded by desire he worked a deal.
In lieu of payment at the time, I asked
him to leave his red silk cord and seal.
The message of my pregnancy soon spread,
and Judah raged, "Let that whore be burned."
So I returned his cord and stopped him dead;
His pride unraveled at the trick I'd turned.
Judah confessed his was the greater blame
because my scheme preserved his family's name.

Rahab, the Harlot

I let them in the house with my own hand
and hid them under bundled stalks of flax.
And when the king sent soldiers to demand
that I release the men, I skewed the facts
to save the Jewish spies with laundered lies.

The news about the parting of the Sea
persuaded me to make these spies my allies,
and so I slept with Canaan's enemy.
"Ruse for ruse. No one in my house dies."
I bargained with the spies and they concurred.
I cast my faith on treason, sex, and lies,
baptizing my behavior as a saboteur.
In my window hung a scarlet cord:
the thread by which my life would be secured.

Ruth, the Moabite

My devotion grew from doubled grief
that filled, then spilled out from my widow's heart
And bound me to Naomi, to live as part
of the Hebrew people and their strange beliefs.
I picked barley, a migrant worker's life,
and the gray–haired landowner took note.
Half my heart said yes and half said no,
but widows' bread came with the role of wife.
I slipped beneath his rough, red blanket in the night,
as Boaz slept alone beside the grain.
Wordlessly I made my offer plain,
Turning death's derisive wrong to right.
It was not love, but fervent loyalty
which gave birth to Jewish royalty.

Bathsheba, the wife of Uriah

Uriah, unsurpassed in loyalty
to Yahweh, to our country and our king,
went off to war with little thought of me,
his wife, alone and childless that warm spring.
While soldiers fought his battles, King David strolled

His roof as I bathed unaware below.
His glance became a gaze. His desire controlled
us both. Trembling, I choked on the word "No."
"I am pregnant," my succinct note read.
His lust descended into crime when he
charged his troops: "I want Uriah dead."
Our baby died, despite our desperate plea.
I reigned as queen in quiet desolation
and saved my tears for hours of isolation.

Blue Irises

She mouths the hymns and the responsive readings
from her wheelchair parked by the second row,
and when the pastor says, "Greet one another
with a holy kiss" folks stretch and stir,
but Evelyn shuts her eyes. She has no need
for this forced, new-fangled fellowship.
At eighty-five, she thinks, "I'm done with kisses"
(Her mother's red lips tatted on her temple,
her father's quick obligatory pecks,
a string of boys with hungry, hollow lips
and sixty years of kisses from a man
all barbed wire and boots).
But this morning, in this country church
the backdoor greeter shuffles down the aisle—
it takes him 90 years—eyes open wide,
he stoops down. His knees crack like gray branches,
and then he smacks his dry lips right on hers.
Her eyes fly open to blue irises
and dust motes floating in the glass-stained light.

Aftermath of a Miracle

Last week's wake is this week's merry-making.
Friends and strangers press inside the house
where Lazarus, the breathing miracle
reclines beside the low–set dinner table.
Martha orders women back and forth
with plates of roasted veal and saffron rice
to serve the Rabbi and his followers.
Men recount, embellishing the news,
Pointing first to Lazarus then Jesus.
From a veiled corner she appears,
Wearing deep green linen, carrying
her dowry in her left arm's graceful curve.
She gazes down at strangers' sandaled feet
as she carves an aisle through the room
to where her brother and the rabbi sprawl.
With care, Mary rests the earthen jar
on the hard floor, lifts her skirt and kneels
next to the guest of honor's naked feet.
He stops mid–conversation as she lifts
the perfume's lid. The costly nuptial
aroma silences the chatty guests.
One by one they turn toward the scene.
She pours the oil over his dusty feet,
then rubs her fingers over callouses,
knobby bones, between his blistered toes:
A muddy anointing for a would-be king.
She stares at him, undoes her chestnut hair
then bows to wipe his feet as if with silk.
The pious and the curious watch with scorn.

Sunday Morning

The two of us, mother and daughter,
meet the two of you, husband
and husband. This is not a stone
cathedral, but a cafe in Soho
where a line of people sprawls
down the walk, around the block.
We greet. A round of hugs and kisses.
We have an appetite for light
and choose the outdoor seating.
As the waiter fills four empty glass,
the ice cubes play like far away chimes.
He leaves a French press on the table.
We talk of travels and vocations.
'Where were you?' one of you asks.
Mercy by the Sea, I say.
'A conference in a convent?'
Skeptical laughter. Eggs arrive.
*I should have tried the cantaloupe
mimosa.* 'Waiter! One mimosa
over here.' The glass appears.
I sip first then pass the glass
round to my left. My daughter takes
a drink and dips a piece of flatbread
into humus. The three of you
discuss remodeling and friends.
You confess: 'I think she
is bat-shit.' then avert your eyes.
We, guilty gossips, agree and nod.
The waiter pours, the water tumbles.

Struck serious, we chew the bread
and pass the glass around again.
Our transgressions dimmed, we sit in silence
at this make-shift altar made
of bread, breath, mercy and mimosas
on a sidewalk in Manhattan.

Hell–Bent

Hallow my eyes
which envy things others possess:
a friend's distinct talent,
a colleague's success.

Hallow my ears
which are deaf to the facts:
the cycle of poverty,
inhumane acts.

Hallow my lips
which embroider a story
to tear others down
and bring myself glory.

Hallow my arms
which are quick to embrace
the lovable, powerful,
but shun the disgraced.

Hallow my feet
which skirt paths of danger,
shirk roads of sacrifice,
and the penniless stranger.

Hallow my heart,
ambiguous, discontent,
doggedly stubborn,
and strangely hell–bent.

Priorities

Leaving

She left her trashcan, contents spilling out.
She left a journal, empty soda cans,
some moldy Starbucks cups, strewn about,
a worn-out backpack, oriental fans.
She left a shampoo bottle, shaving cream,
socks and Nikes on the bathroom floor,
her favorite sweater, torn along a seam,
a box of thank you notes behind the door.
I found her jeans from twenty pounds ago,
forgotten formals hanging in her closet,
mementos of the boys she used to know.
Discarded classics, a valuable deposit.
She took the lamp I use to read at night;
So now I read by dim, anemic light.

Mac and Cheese

He's her mac, and she's his cheese.
He's the strings on her guitar.
She's the sunshine; he's the breeze.
He's her fan; she'll be his star.
She doubts herself; he'll push her far.
She's got piercings, he, tattoos.
Nineteen's got nothing much to lose.

He makes sauce, and she adds spice.
She's the holes in his old jeans.
He's rock steady; she thinks twice.
They both spring from sturdy genes,
But taking vows while in their teens?
He makes pesto (is she nuts?).
They'll need love and luck and guts.

Defying Nature

"Two adults," I say and hand the woman
a twenty and a five. "Too much," she says.
"Mom, I've got something that I want to say."
I retrieve the five, nodding in thanks.
"I don't believe in God," he says too loudly.
The clerk freezes, the twenty in mid-air.
"OK," I look at him.
                      "Do I get change?"
I ask the clerk who stares, holding the bill.
"Did you hear me, Mom?" his voice is thin.
"Yes, I did and said that it's OK,"
The line of patrons rustles behind us.
Slowly, slowly the clerk hands me two dollars,
and we walk through the turnstile.
                    "Is that all?"
he says. "Just, OK?"
                    "Yes, I think that's all."
We stroll through the huge, hewn gem exhibit.
I study an amethyst and think it odd,
he chose the Natural History Museum
to tell me he does not believe in God.

String Theory

The cry from meadowlark to meadowlark,
the sigh and creak of time-worn hard-wood stairs,
all play on strings much smaller than a quark.
Strings produce pollution in the air,
Give rise to windstorms, hail, and thunder-snow,
and serve September's vegetable fare.
Minute strings lend fireflies their glow,
make up the composition of our genes,
and modulate your affable hello.
Strings zip shut the sides of green wax beans,
dangle shiny carrots, tether kites,
and stitch together seams of denim jeans.
Strings turn on and off electric lights,
close and open windows, screens and doors,
and warm up living rooms on winter nights.
If subatomic strings pull tides to shores,
does unseen matter draw my heart to yours?

The Memory of Her Melody

At first her voice, her melody
took over very quietly.
It tiptoed barefoot down the halls
then penetrated through the walls.
It spread itself across the floor
then softly slipped beneath my door.
Her grace notes, swift, like fireflies,
danced around before my eyes.
All day, all night soprano sound
Crescendoed up, then gently down.
The song grew rich, robust and strong,
Yet I, in secret, came to long
for quiet hours and empty space.
Then soon her voice outgrew the place.
Her melody packed up its things,
and suddenly it sprouted wings.
It quickly flew straight out the door
and rarely enters anymore.
The house is quiet, huge and cold
and I, alone, am growing old.

The Lovers' Knot

Mere child's play. Simply, with delight,
by placing right on left, and left on right
we interlaced our two unseasoned strands,
then with a tug, a knot was in our hands.
At first it held together tension free.
Our strands, though twined, moved independently.
Then culture shock pulled one strand east, one west,
Our progeny increased the strain: a test.
The tasks of separate callings now divide
and yank each strand to its opposing side.
The ends are frayed, the lines are wholly taut,
but tension formed an everlasting knot.
At thirty years, the strands hold strong, secure,
inseparable and certain to endure.

Priorities

I graded essays from last week.
We made a quick trip to the store.
You read John's Gospel in the Greek.
I mopped the hardwood kitchen floor.
You sat and paid the bills on-line.
I placed clean t-shirts in your drawer.
You organized your books, then mine.
I sent a message to the kids.
You tied the fence with baling twine.
I matched containers to their lids.
You sorted clothes to get rid of.
We double-checked our eBay bids.
We've finished all the chores above.
What's that? You're bored? We could make love.

Live Life Away

I stand in the room where we dined life away.
Three ghosts meet me here to restage our old play.
One flies to the basement and tunes up a bass,
then sound underscores the bright scenes taking place:
a brother and sister baptizing a cat,
a young teenage girl in a green faded hat,
a Thanksgiving table with turkey and ham,
green Jell-O for Chuck, rolls and raspberry jam.
I enter the kitchen where children who chatter
draw pictures with crayons. Their dim voices scatter.
The ghosts lead the way up the stairs to the place
where we dreamed life away. A forgotten embrace
from earlier days is perfuming the air.
A Wrinkle in Time and a boy's night time prayer
whisper together, and I am aware
that a redheaded bride stands before a large mirror.
She smiles in the glass and says, "Mommy, come nearer."
I cry, "I am coming!"—but then she is gone.
So I walk to the rail and the ghosts draw me on
to the now empty room where we lived life away.
You each left before me, and this is the day
that I must leave too. We now live life apart.
But you know, wherever you go, if my heart
were a house, you'd be home.

Rosary 2.0

I imagine
that I hold
a sphere of air
where love sits
rocking in
a wooden chair,
where kindness cups
each chin, and joy
pecks every cheek,
and peace spins
soundlessly
around within.
Then, I imagine
you are there.
Oh, Lord,
hear my prayer.

Through the Window

The juniper surrenders to the weight
of winter. It lies prostrate, pointing south,
buried beneath the season's icy freight.
The snow-drowned trunk, each ice-bound twig and bough
signal this pine's inevitable fate.
I watch its solemn bend, its reverent bow,
its mysteriously yielding peace,
as its berries drop, dying to increase.

Summer's End

The aspen trees are hinting gold,
yet fall has made no grave advances.
It's August now. The summer's old.

Colors turn, but they're not bold
enough for autumn's dying dances.
The aspen trees are hinting gold.

The robins leave their homes unsold.
No more shrill high-pitched romances.
It's August now. The summer's old.

The sun retains her shimmering hold
though her trajectory's askance.
The aspen trees are hinting gold.

But I'm a fool who pans for gold
in unlikely circumstances.
It's August now. The summer's old.

Autumn has a mere toehold,
at summer's end wait second chances.
The aspen trees are hinting gold.
It's August now. The summer's old.

Where Dreams Comingle with Dust

Twilight

I can't recall how I got here,
by light year leap or slow, dead creep?
First minute, hour, day, then year,
I can't recall how I got here.
The details blur, then disappear.
I dreamed my life in twilight sleep.
I can't recall how I got here,
by light year leap or slow, dead creep?

Dust

She turned to the right
where the space spills wide
and the fields sit fallow,
where green bleeds to brown
and wind rips the brush,
where faces float in clouds
and air smells of nothingness,
where cardinals sing doleful songs
and coyotes skulk at dusk,
where midnight swallows the stars
and afternoon scolds the eyes,
where burrs stick to soles
and dreams comingle with dust,
where empty air dries skin
and leaves its ashen traces,
where water tastes of rust
and salt has no savor,
where love has grown sour
and the world spins wrong.

Faces of the Enemy

She goes everywhere I go,
a well-disguised, chic enemy.
She's my level-headed foe.

When I wake up at five, I know
she'll hand a list of "shoulds" to me.
She goes everywhere I go.

Without her prodding, I'd grow slow,
neglect responsibility.
She's my reasonable foe.

If not for her, I might let go,
give in to spontaneity.
She goes everywhere I go.

I might forget the debts I owe
and live each day as if I'm free,
but she's a false, smooth-talking foe.

I might make angels in the snow,
but I'm bred for anxiety.
She goes everywhere I go,
my mendacious, two-faced foe.

Royal Revenge

The crux of it? I would love to hate you:
for purposefully spoiling English class,
for making teaching so damn hard to do,
for your false veneer of charm, your comments—crass,
surreptitious like a poison gas,
for your capacity to spin the truth,
and for your spend-thrift attitude toward youth.

I would love to hate you, Andrew Stone,
for mocking poems, books, and a Shakespeare play,
for your sense of self-importance—overblown—
for ripping up your graded essay
and shouting, "What the fuck!" at me today.
I should hate you, but my heart simply can't.
My payback is this rhythmic, royal rant.

Your Name Is Seth

You're Elbert County born and bred.
You're loud and burly. You wear Red.
You seldom show your winsome smile—
That might destroy your tough-guy style,
So you hand out high fives instead.

You're boisterous ways leave things unsaid.
Fierce lineman, stories of your feats have spread,
But, son, in you "there is no guile."
Your name is Seth.

How quickly your bright season fled,
Followed by doubts of what's ahead:
With all your might you'd move the pile;
But my classroom is your longest mile.
You're a champion, trust your head.
Your name is Seth.

A Narrative in Need of Words

Anika, why are you crying?
She has no words. Between us is her paper,
her silence, and her tears. She shakes her head.
This is hard.
My words punctuate the silence
Thesis, content, grammar, syntax, style.
Do you have any questions?
No, she shakes her head.
I offer the subjunctive:
If you take this to the Writing Lab,
a tutor will help you.
I watch this girl of too few words
fade from an office chair into the rain.
I blame her high school teachers,
I curse the university.
This problem is systemic.
When there is not a soul to hear, I say
Maybe she is just as dumb as dirt,
I take a Tylenol PM and go to bed.
That night I dream I'm reading her revision
and when I try to speak no sound comes out.
Awake, I click the only words I have:
Dear Anika,
    I did not know how
To help you. I am sorry. Can we meet
again next Monday after class?
My paltry olive branch heartens her.
Anika arrives, revision in hand.
She smiles, takes a seat and says

How was your weekend?
She passes me the paper and I skim
The jumbled syntax and the misused phrases.
I stall with random questions
Where is home?
I wonder at her surge of words—
Adopted from an orphanage
when I was eight years old.
No Russian, only a few words.
She visits the Writing Lab three times,
twice we meet again.

Her skills increase by trickling increments.
When Anika falters through her speech,
the class applauds and whistles.
If *pass* and *fail* are verbs,
    I cannot find their agents.
Syntax slurs. Definitions blur.
This is hard. I have no words.

Fool

Don't write about the moon—
overdone,
too often sung.

Don't rhyme
of her banality
as she twirls in perigee.

Don't versify
the humors of
her waxing, waning love.

Don't tell the lunar tale
of her desire
to light the sea on fire.

Don't trace her ivory face.
Resist her pull,
don't be a fool.

Occupied

There's pansies, that's for thoughts. Ophelia

Today a purple
platoon stands
at attention,
trimmed in violet,
a shock of yellow
at the core.
These humble warriors
now occupy
my garden's borders
which yesterday
were idle plains
of hardened earth,
and my midwinter
mind surrenders
to spindly-legged soldiers
bearing masses
of strategic,
velvet weapons.

Lilac Gowns

No pleasantries. Six women wait, alone.
Unalike save for the clinic gown.
One taps her toe, a sandaled metronome.
One quickly flips through *Time*, her head bent down.
A wall of water dives through pastel green,
inside a room of vulnerable breasts.
One fears she has a cancer gene,
a heartbreak that her history suggests.
One remembers infants' greedy lips,
mornings half-asleep and milk-white nights.
They all recall their lovers' fingertips
and conjure scenes of jeopardized delights.
They breathe the common air. They wait. They turn
away from eyes that mirror their concern.

Mosca Pass Trail to the Great Sand Dunes

Each grain of sand conspired to draw her down
the hard-packed gravel trail cut through the canyon.
She felt its pull, that desert sea of brown
with undulating tide. With firm abandon
she hiked down. The summer was too young
for graceful lupine and demure bell flowers,
only prickly cacti bloomed and flung
their crimson lot in with the dune-field's powers.
The fissures and the fault lines ran along
rock walls. What caused those cracks? She wasn't sure.
An unknown bird beguiled her with its song.
In two hours' time, she reached the gritty shore,
and there she sank ankle-deep in sand,
no map, and nothing left on which to stand.

Rattled

She opened her mouth
and the truth fell out

A thud, a crack,
no getting it back

Syllables in flight,
lambent white

A naked word,
shocking, when heard

Skin quivered,
a spine shivered

The feral truth,
with a mind of its own

Shook her brains
and rattled her bones

Return

I have resisted.
I chose to be alone,
but, Darling, I admit
my words were cold, hard stone.
Return.
You've been gone for days.
Come back. I long to learn
your fiery, wanton ways.
So run your tongue inside my ear,
your fickle fingers down
my spine.
Untie my gown,
my mind.
Without your fire,
my words are dour,
the frigid kind.

Meteor

Tonight's dark moon blacks out the countryside
and veils the miles of taut barbed wire fence.
It envelops Angus steer and hides
the bales of hay beneath its blue-black tents.
The truant moon conceals the points of light
from far-off suns. A driver grips a wheel,
and tires cling to double lines of white.
She inches, purblind, through the black surreal.
Then for an instant, fire turns night to day
as an orange torch streaks through the skies.
The tragic ending of a brilliant play.
Sparks trail the plunging fire as it dies.
A meteor flames out, light years from home,
and ignites the lonesome kindling of her bones.

Epistle

Your kind is ubiquitous.
You ascend to limbs and ledges,
six red toes gripping lofty edges,
to get a god's-eye view of us.
Your black-hole eyes and down-curved beak
are ringed and splashed with bright turquoise.
Your plump, round body sails with poise
into the blue, a pastel streak,
as white-tipped wings sharply whistle
your plainsong of austerity
and fluttering sincerity.
Be mindful of Earth's sludge and thistles.
Brown-breasted laureate perched above,
lament our sorrows, Mourning Dove.

A Word

It was a word that hurled
each star into its space,
A word that gave the world
its form, the moon its face,
a word that shaped the trees,
and raised up land from seas.

It was a word that turned
a light on in the sky,
A word from which birds learned
to chirp, the wind to sigh.
A word rained down on plants
and proffered music, dance.

It was a word that stirred
the life into each creature,
A quiet word conferred
a grace into each feature.
The cosmos, shining, stood;
the understatement: "Good."

Beyond All Bearing

Turning

This is the season of turning and tears,
Emerald aspens have grieved themselves gold.
The sepia moon dips down closely and hears
The sighs of the season of turning and tears.
This blue planet spins and tallies her years,
Young bones have gone cold and will never grow old.
This is the season of turning and tears,
Emerald aspens have grieved themselves gold.

Honeysuckle

They walked in pairs
searching north to south
and south to north
along the highway's shoulder
where the scent of honeysuckle hung

The younger sister swore that she would find him
a patch of tamped down grass her clue
she knew, she knew
she knew

9-1-1
the sirens screamed
the searchers gathered at the scene

The older sister stepped up to the guardrail
—as firstborns do—
and gazed between the leafy branches
It's only sisters now
A twig of hope
snapped in two

(I hovered over wild grass
and above damp ground
below the tree tops
When I saw you
when I heard you cry
I cried too
Then I swept up and eastward
silently and free,
Forgive me.)

The men saw all
that they were trained to see:
a thin young man,
belt around his neck
chin down
knees planted in the ground
face marred by insects
body bloated
sodden by the summer rain
no ligature marks
no evidence of struggle
no broken bones
no foul play
all in a detective's day

Don't look—
You don't want to see
said the sheriff with the shiny forehead
as his minions wagged their heads

Who are you,
to tell me
what I do or do not want to see?
she spat and sparked
a fire in the air

One detective stepped over the rail
When you say 'ready,'
I will move this branch
he whispered, motioning

Yes. Now.

She saw his body
perfectly,
as a mother sees

Time wrinkled,
as scene by scene,
the boy tumbled across
her memory's silver screen

She saw him years ago
blonde head bowed
pink knees on the basement's cold cement
small hands clasped
she heard his first impromptu prayer:
Thank you, God,
for turning on the light

Breathing in the holy
scent of honeysuckle,
she stumbled into night.

Like the Wedding Supper of the Lamb

for David Solomito and Dane Larsen

The day the enemy eclipsed the sun,
we stumbled on the highway's gravel shoulder,
tongue-tied, numb, cold, growing colder.
The adversary seemingly had won.
Tall grass bowed down. Deep called out to deep,
and miles away, you heard our nascent cry,
lighting candles to remand the sunless sky.
In death's presence, you prepared a feast.
The city's air slipped through the open window,
Orange flames grew tall, you poured more wine,
A hint of chopped mint calmed us as we dined.
Below us, the East River steadied its flow.
You gave us one warm evening of relief,
as we wander through this glacial grief.

Actuary Tables

It was not the fact that he was dead,
not the details that the sheriff shared,
not the frayed backpack scattering
her boy's pen and journal on the table.
Nor was it the fact that he would never
marry, cut a vinyl record, father
his own boy, or grow old gradually.
Facts were not what knocked her to her knees,
not what sucked the air out of her lungs.
It was the probability that she
would live another thirty years, the chance
that she would almost certainly survive.

the thin place

whatever separates the here from there,
the now from next, grow thin until they merge

he and she stand planted in that place,
not earth, nor air, not wondering where

she stares at him, as light from somewhere, something
not the sun, sparkles on his glasses' frames

she knows that red and blue plaid flannel shirt,
those hazel eyes, green pools with flecks of truth

tears move calmly down his cheeks, his voice
retains its gentleness, its thorn, its honey

grace dissolves her thick and foggy grief
and fuels her flight across that lucid place

with her right hand, she clasps his left forearm,
his slender bones, the warm and threadbare flannel

when they touch, love like lightening surges,
but with that touch the here and there unmerges

Paper Whites / December

Bulbs—these dun, dormant gifts.
The very word bursts from my mouth,
my breathe rushes past my lips—
I bury five, homely rounds
inside glass houses filled with rock
and water.
    I blink once, twice,
and roots shoot between the rocks.
The globes bulge, split and spit
grassy spears toward the light.
I turn my back, they sprout by inches.
They rush, swell, burst, bow,
and bear white blinding blossoms
on stubborn stalks that pulse with life.

Crossing

Like a silken scrim, the morning rain
falls straight, dotted with flecks of ashy
snow. I run toward the Queensborough Bridge
and join this morning's moving human line.
Cold drops roll down my nose and scatter
as I find my pace on this day's run,

my post-dawn office: Wake. Remember. Run.
West into Manhattan in the rain,
cyclists are few. A sorry, smaller scatter
of people walk this concrete path of ash.
My grief and I run right side of the line.
A woman wails a blues tune from the bridge.

Puddles inches deep swell on the bridge.
It's difficult to navigate this run,
carrying you. I thump over the line.
A cyclist shouts over trains, trucks, and rain
and shoos me back. My grief, like kicked up ash,
unsettles. Blistering embers fly and scatter.

Umbrellas and bright raincoats scatter
to cubicles the west end of the bridge.
I run east again, chasing ashen
shades of you, my son. I run and run,
but you elude me in this morning rain.
Protocol should rule this human line.

You crossed that line.
Your lyrics stick to me. Your songs don't scatter.

They sing louder than this morning's rain
and glaze my gooseflesh. I know no bridge
leads me to you or you to me. I run.
This morning's office tastes of song and ash.

You chose. You turned yourself to dust and ash.
Still, I choose this morning's humming line.
I wake, and I remember you, and run.
Your choice dams up my breath. I must scatter
what I cannot bear across this bridge,
as I run my office in the rain.

I sift through ash, what to keep? to scatter?
I step out of line atop this bridge. I pause,
I scatter dust and ash and run home in rain.

Tender

". . . the girl got up and began to walk about" Mark 5:42

Forgive me, Son, it's time for me to go.
I have sat among the feverfew
beside this tree, the spot your spirit flew.
Like Jairus, I believed, but God was slow.
Your death short-circuited the sun and stars.
Noon was night. There was no lambent moon.
Yet Earth sustained her circuit and her spin—
Asters. Oak leaves. Hail. Tears. Snow.
Twice I sat the calendar around.
Then, a match-sized torch burned in my night,
and a tiny cloud reflected light.
I cursed that tree and got up from the ground.
You did not rise and walk. God is slow
and slowly tenders me the strength to go.

Rainlight

Myrrh and aloes balm the morning air.
Their yellow residue coats Mary's hands,
the body she anointed is now gone.
An inkling in her soul bids her remain.
Muted rainlight shrouds the garden-tomb.
A man emerges from the rainlight's fog
and smells the burial fragrance on her hands.
Age-old olive trees lean in to watch.
The stranger speaks her name: "Mary. Mary."
Then traces her cheek—two angels hold their breath—
He gently cups her chin in his right hand.
Her equilibrium flags, and she wobbles.
"Mary," a name as common as the rain,
echoes through her bones and through the tomb.
"Rabbi!" she gasps and stretches out her hands.
The weight of grief slips from the woman's palms.
Beneath the olive trees two angels quiver.
the fog fails, and rainlight's canopy lifts.

Consider These Lilies

Jesus' tears, salty liquid seeds,
burrowed deep into Gethsemane's ground
and lay to rest inside a loamy grave.
A patch of earth became a burial mound.
Dirt's dominion did its work on tears,
turning them to roots and bulbs which burst
the rocky ceiling of the hard-packed soil,
and tender stalks sprang up, spines straight, headfirst.
Now they thrive, bright offspring of agony.
Their perennial blooms climb verdant ladders
like ivory-robed apostles, open-mouthed,
or brassy trumpets sounding weighty matters.
Consider these lilies, how they simply bloom,
regaled with glory and heady, thick perfume.

Beyond All Bearing

In winter, when pines weary,
when aligned limbs quiver with longing,
and the ground moans under gravity's weight,
it's then, through the northern night
that concentric silver circles radiate
like wind-borne waves racing shoreward,
beautiful beyond all bearing.
    Swifter still—
God speeds across the cosmos
earthward, arms open wide.

www.ingramcontent.com/pod-product-compliance
Lightning Source LLC
Chambersburg PA
CBHW060420090426
42734CB00011B/2388